CELEBRATING THE CITY OF HA LONG

Celebrating the City of Ha Long

Walter the Educator

Silent King Books

SILENT KING BOOKS

SKB

Copyright © 2024 by Walter the Educator

All rights reserved. No part of this book may be reproduced in any manner whatsoever without written permission except in the case of brief quotations embodied in critical articles and reviews.

First Printing, 2024

Disclaimer
This book is a literary work; the story is not about specific persons, locations, situations, and/or circumstances unless mentioned in a historical context. Any resemblance to real persons, locations, situations, and/or circumstances is coincidental. This book is for entertainment and informational purposes only. The author and publisher offer this information without warranties expressed or implied. No matter the grounds, neither the author nor the publisher will be accountable for any losses, injuries, or other damages caused by the reader's use of this book. The use of this book acknowledges an understanding and acceptance of this disclaimer.

Celebrating the City of Ha Long is a little collectible souvenir book that belongs to the Celebrating Cities Book Series by Walter the Educator. Collect them all and more books at WaltertheEducator.com

USE THE EXTRA SPACE TO TAKE NOTES AND DOCUMENT YOUR MEMORIES

HA LONG

Emerald waves whisper secrets through limestone veins,

Celebrating the City of
Ha Long

Ha Long Bay, where legends rise and ebb with the tide,

Guardians of stone, ancient and wise,

Watch over a paradise, where earth and sky collide.

From the dawn's gentle touch, light awakens mist,

A delicate veil over jade waters persists.

Islands like sentinels, steadfast and grand,

Tell tales of dragons, of heaven's command.

In the early morn, the fishermen set sail,

Their laughter mingles with the seabirds' wail.

Wooden boats dance upon the bay's serene face,

Celebrating the City of Ha Long

Carving paths through silence, an ethereal grace.

Caves like hidden cathedrals, secretive, vast,

Echoes of time in each shadow they cast.

Stalactites drip stories from their ancient tongues,

Songs of creation, of battles once sung.

Emerald eyes of the ocean, you hold a mystique,

A tranquil realm where the heart can speak.

In the embrace of your islands, solace is found,

A sanctuary where peace is the only sound.

Celebrating the City of Ha Long

Lanterns glow softly as dusk turns to night,

Casting dreams in the bay, shimmering bright.

Lovers walk hand in hand by the shore,

Wrapped in the magic, craving nothing more.

The city hums a melody of modern and past,

Skyscrapers rise where memories last.

Markets alive with colors, scents, and sound,

A symphony of culture, rich and profound.

Children play under the banyan trees' shade,

Their laughter a testament to the life you've made.

Elders gather, sharing tales with pride,

Of Ha Long's glory, a heritage wide.

Temples and pagodas, humble and grand,

Offer solace to the soul, a spiritual stand.

Incense swirls, prayers ascend to the sky,

In this sacred harmony, the soul learns to fly.

Emerald dreams in the morning light,

In Ha Long Bay, where day meets night.

A place where the soul finds its way,

In the beauty of Ha Long, night and day.

Celebrating the City of Ha Long

ABOUT THE CREATOR

Walter the Educator is one of the pseudonyms for Walter Anderson. Formally educated in Chemistry, Business, and Education, he is an educator, an author, a diverse entrepreneur, and he is the son of a disabled war veteran. "Walter the Educator" shares his time between educating and creating. He holds interests and owns several creative projects that entertain, enlighten, enhance, and educate, hoping to inspire and motivate you. Follow, find new works, and stay up to date with
Walter the Educator™ at
WaltertheEducator.com.

www.ingramcontent.com/pod-product-compliance
Lightning Source LLC
LaVergne TN
LVHW010622070526
838199LV00063BA/5228